*Daughter, you have always been
a wonderful source of joy to me.
You have touched my life
with a magic all your own...
I want you to know that the love we share
has made being a parent the greatest feeling
I have ever known.*
— Deanna Beisser

# For You, My Daughter

### ...Poems to Say How Much I Love You

A Special Blue Mountain Arts® Collection

**Blue Mountain Press** ™

SPS Studios, Inc., Boulder, Colorado

*Library of Congress Catalog Card Number: 00-011344*
*ISBN: 0-88396-571-2*

*Manufactured in China*
*Second Printing: March 2001*

*This book is printed on recycled paper.*

### Library of Congress Cataloging-in-Publication Data

*For you, my daughter : poems that say how much I love you: a special Blue Mountain Arts collection.*
    *p. cm.*
   *ISBN 0-88396-571-2 (alk. paper)*

  *1. Mothers and daughters–Poetry. 2. Fathers and daughters–Poetry. 3. American poetry–20th century. 4. Daughters–Poetry, I. SPS Studios (Firm)*
  *PS595.M65 F67 2000*
  *811.008'03520441–dc21*                    *00-011344*

                                            *CIP*

# SPS Studios, Inc.
P.O. Box 4549, Boulder, Colorado 80306

# Contents

# Daughter, I Will Always
# Be Here with Love for You

Did you know that I loved you long before you were born?
When I first held you in my arms,
one of my childhood dreams came true.
I remember staring at your perfect little features
and feeling thrilled at each new sound and expression.
A fierce need to protect you came over me then,
and it has never gone away.
When you were a child,
I was able to hold you close through illness and heartache.
I could hold your hand as you faced new experiences,
and my presence and guidance seemed to
assure you of a certain level of safety.
But little by little, I have had to let you go
and allow you to make your own way.
So often I wanted to call you back and have you stay
in the protective circle of my arms.
I never wanted you to have to face injury or heartache,
yet I knew that you had to in order to grow.
Now you are making your own decisions.
Just remember that no matter what, I love you.
I could never stop loving you.
You are the hugs and smiles from my past,
the hopes and dreams of my future.
Take care, my daughter, and know that you are never alone.
We are connected by the strongest bond there is:
the love between parent and child.

— Barbara Cage

# My Wish for You, Daughter

*I can't give you the world,*
*filled with all its riches.*
*I can't promise you a life*
*free from sickness, pain,*
*and disappointment,*
*for that is a gift not mine to give.*
*I cannot guarantee that you*
*will never feel your heart break.*
*My only wish for you*
*is that you fulfill the dreams*
*deep within you...*

*I wish for you to know yourself*
*and be faithful to yourself.*
*For if you do,*
*you will be able to fully love others.*
*Be free to choose your course in life*
*without fearing a wrong decision.*
*Reflect on what you have been taught,*
*and take time to listen to your heart.*
*Never lose the ability to feel with open arms*
*all the passion and joy that life holds for you.*
*Give all you have*
*without looking for something in return.*
*Reach out for that which you can attain*
*and not for that which is impossible.*
*I wish for you, my daughter,*
*to be all you can,*
*for only then will you awaken*
*to the person you want to be.*

*— Joan Benicken*

*When you are happy,*
  *I'll love you with*
    *a joyful heart.*
*When you are sad,*
  *I'll love you with a heart*
  *made a little heavier*
    *by your tears.*
*When you are right,*
  *I'll love you with a heart*
    *filled with pride.*
*When you are wrong,*
  *I'll love you with a heart*
    *that has learned acceptance.*
*When you succeed,*
  *I'll love you with*
    *a cheering heart.*
*When you fail,*
  *I'll love you with a heart*
    *that rewards the efforts you've made.*
*When you dream,*
  *I'll love you with*
    *an encouraging heart.*
*When you give up,*
  *I'll love you with a heart*
    *that is strong enough for both of us.*
*When you are simply you,*
*in whatever mood or phase of your life,*
  *I'll love you with all my heart*
    *and more than you'll ever know.*

*— Linda Sackett-Morrison*

9

# To My Daughter, I Love You

When you were born
I held you in my arms
and just kept smiling at you
You always smiled back
your big eyes wide open
full of love
You were such a
beautiful
good
sweet baby
Now
as I watch you grow up
and become your own person
I look at you
your laughter
your happiness
your simplicity
your beauty

*And I know that you will*
*be able to enjoy a life*
*of sensitivity*
*goodness*
*accomplishment*
*and love*
*in a world that hopefully is at peace*
*I want to tell you that*
*I am so proud of you*
*and I dearly*
*love you*

— Susan Polis Schutz

# Daughter,
# I Want You to Know...

*It's hard sometimes, when people
are changing their lives, to
understand each other, or even
to talk. You are struggling right
now for independence and the
right to live your own way...
and I sometimes struggle for
the strength to let you do it.
I wish now and then for the days
when a kiss or a hug could make
your world bright again; but
your world is more difficult now,
and you want to make your own
way in it — which is as it should be.
I only want you to know...
that when you get hurt, I will
hurt for you; and that deep
down, I always have confidence
in your ability to find your place
in your world. If you ever need a
caring heart, or someone to listen
to your deepest dreams or concerns,
I will be there for you;
and remember, above all else...
that I love and care for you.*

*— M. Joye*

# You're a Very Special Person

*Carry the sun inside you,*
*and reach out for the dreams that guide you.*
*You have everything you need to take*
*you where you want to go.*
*You have abilities and talents*
*and attributes that belong to you alone,*
*and you have what it takes to make*
*your path of success... lead to happiness.*

*You're a very special person.*
*You have qualities that get better every day!*
*You have the courage and strength to see*
*    things through.*
*You have smiles that will serve as your guides.*
*You have a light that will shine in you*
*     'til the end of time.*
*You have known the truth of yesterday,*
*    and you have an inner map that will*
*    lead the way to a very beautiful tomorrow.*
*You have gifts that have never even been opened*
*    and personal journeys waiting to be explored.*
*You have so much going for you.*
*You are a special person, and you have a*
*    future that is in the best of hands.*
*    And you need to remember: If you have*
*    plans you want to act on and dreams*
*    you've always wanted to come true...*

*You have what it takes, because...*
*    You*
*        have*
*            you.*
*                    — Douglas Pagels*

*Did you know,*
  *sweet daughter of mine,*
*That my world changed forever*
*When you came into my life?*
*No one could have prepared me*
  *for the depth of love*
*That sprang into my heart for you*
*From the very moment you were born.*
*And I continually think of ways*
  *I can let you know*
*How very special you are to me.*
*You truly are a treasure,*
*And I will cherish you all of my life.*
*I will brag about you and show you off*
*Every time I get the chance.*
*And though I don't know how*
  *it's possible,*
*You become more dear to me*
*With every year that passes by.*

— Cheryl Barker

# In Case I Haven't
# Told You Lately...

*Many days go by and I find myself saying*
*the same things to you day in and day out:*
*"Clean your room."*
*"Is your room clean?"*
*"Do your homework."*
*"Did you finish your homework?"*
*"Don't be late."*
*"Take the trash out, please..."*

*Many nights, after you have*
*fallen asleep and look so peaceful,*
*I have wondered to myself...*
*Did I tell you that I love you?*
*That I appreciate all you do for me?*
*That through your entire life*
*you will find me in your cheering section?*
*Have I asked you lately about your happiness*
*and what's going on in your life?*

*I am sorry that there are so many times*
*when I get caught up with the everyday routines*
*that I forget the simple, important things in life.*
*I hope that you will forgive me for my shortcomings,*
*as I will forgive you.*
*Always remember that*
*no matter how busy I seem to be,*
*I love you very much,*
*and I am proud of all that you do*
*and all that you stand for.*

*— Toni Crossgrove Shippen*

*Daughter, you have always been*
*a wonderful source of joy to me.*
*You have touched my life*
*with a magic all your own.*
*There were times when you struggled with me,*
*longing for your own independence*
*and searching for your own place in the world.*
*I remember those times as*
*I tried to hold you close*
*and hold on tightly to my little girl,*
*knowing all the time in my heart that*
*it was a part of growing up for you and for me,*
*a part of life we would endure*
*and eventually become closer than ever before.*
*You are more than a dream come true for me:*
*you are a part of my life that will carry on.*
*And as I watch you changing,*
*I see a special happiness in all that you do.*
*With my heart full of memories,*
*I want you to know that the love we share*
*has made being a parent the greatest feeling*
*I have ever known.*

— *Deanna Beisser*

*I* hope that today
   and always
the love I have for you
is reaching out
and touching you –
    making your days
      a little brighter
   and your heart
      a little warmer.

I hope that today
   and always
you are aware of how
special you are to me,
and how lucky I feel
   to have you in my life.

      – Susie Schneider

*I* ask myself
  why I have been
    blessed with someone
    so understanding
    and so caring...
Perhaps it's because
I can truly appreciate you
or maybe it's because
   God knew
   I needed you
   so much.

      – Jean Therese Lynch

# May There Always Be Happiness in Your Life

*H*appiness *cannot come from without.*
*It must come from within. It is not what we*
*see and touch or that which others do for us*
*which makes us happy; it is that which we*
*think and feel and do, first for the other*
*fellow and then for ourselves.*

*– Helen Keller*

*K*eep
*your face to*
        *the sunshine*
*and you cannot*
        *see the shadow.*

*– Helen Keller*

# Don't Ever...

Don't ever try to understand everything –
some things will just never make sense.
Don't ever be reluctant to show your feelings –
when you're happy, give in to it!
When you're not, live with it.
Don't ever be afraid to try to make things better –
you might be surprised at the results.
Don't ever take the weight of the world
on your shoulders.
Don't ever feel threatened by the future –
take life one day at a time.
Don't ever feel guilty about the past –
what's done is done. Learn from any mistakes
you might have made.
Don't ever feel that you are alone –
there is always somebody there for you
to reach out to.
Don't ever forget that you can achieve
so many of the things you can imagine –
imagine that! It's not as hard as it seems.
Don't ever stop loving,
don't ever stop believing,
don't ever stop dreaming your dreams.

— Laine Parsons

# My Dear Daughter...

*I know I am critical of you sometimes, but it's only because I have experienced so much more of life, and I can often see that the path you are taking today may not take you to where you want to be tomorrow.*

*I know, too, that you still have to experience life for yourself. If I can, I just want to spare you some of the pain I had to go through on my own path in life...*

*When the words don't come with all I want to say, I can still say this: I love you tremendously. I would do anything for you. And I promise I will try to be more patient and understanding of you, and I pray that you will do the same for me.*

*And do me a favor sometimes... tell me you love me, okay? Having you grow up so quickly is hard on me.*

*– Carol Ann Bader*

# It's Up to You to Make Your Life the Best It Can Be

*This life is the only one you're given.*
*Look for opportunities to grow,*
*and never be discouraged*
*in your efforts to do so.*
*Replace your weaknesses with positives;*
*take life's broken pieces*
*and re-create your dreams.*
*Never measure the future by the past;*
*let yesterday become a memory*
*and tomorrow a promise.*
*Begin each day by focusing*
*on all that is good,*
*and you'll be in a position*
*to handle whatever comes along.*
*Take responsibility for your actions;*
*never make excuses*
*for not being the best you can be.*
*If you should slip,*
*be comforted by the thought*
*that we all do at times.*
*Determine your tomorrow*
*by the choices you make today,*
*and you'll find yourself living*
*in joy and triumph.*

*– Linda E. Knight*

# Whenever Life Is Getting You Down, Daughter, Remember This...

To solve each problem one at a time;
to take each day as it comes.
To stick to your goals, no matter
        what happens,
and press on toward your dreams.
To keep your attention focused on
        the future,
as you consider the solutions at hand.
To look for the bright side,
even though it may be temporarily
        covered by a cloud.
To smile often, even when a frown
        feels more natural.
To think of those you love,
        and know that they love you, too.

No matter how difficult it may seem,
you have within you the power,
        the ability,
            and the knowledge
        to make things better.

                                    – Lindsay Newman

*Your life can be*
*what you want it to be...*
*You'll make it through*
*whatever comes along.*

*Within you are so many answers.*
*Understand, have courage,*
*be strong.*

— *Douglas Pagels*

*When you encounter difficulties and*
*contradictions, do not try to break*
*them, but bend them with gentleness*
*and time.*

— *St. Francis de Sales*

# Daughter, You Are Loved

When the road seems too long
When darkness sets in
When everything turns out wrong
And you can't find a friend
Remember - you are loved

When smiles are hard to come by
And you're feeling down
When you spread your wings to fly
And can't get off the ground
Remember – you are loved

When time runs out before you're through
And it's over before you begin
When little things get to you
And you just can't win
Remember – you are loved

When your loved ones are far away
And you are on your own
When you don't know what to say
When you're afraid of being alone
Remember – you are loved

When your sadness comes to an end
And everything is going right
May you think of your family and friends
And keep their love in sight
A thank-you for being loved

May you see the love around you
In everything you do
And when troubles seem to surround you
May all the love shine through
You are blessed – you are loved

– Roger Pinches

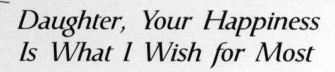

# Daughter, Your Happiness Is What I Wish for Most

*I wish for you to always see the goodness*
*in this world,*
*to do your part in helping those*
*less fortunate,*
*to walk hand in hand with those*
*of less talent,*
*to follow those of more knowledge,*
*to be an equal with those who are different.*

*I wish for you to find your special purpose*
*in this world so full of choices*
*and to help lead those who stray.*
*I wish for you to become your own*
*individual, to set yourself apart from*
*those who are the same.*

*I wish for you the self-confidence*
*to say no when it is necessary*
*and the strength to stand alone.*

I wish for you the approval of yourself
  to love and respect everything that
    you are and will become.
I wish for you to reap the fruits
  of your talents,
to walk with pride down the road of life,
to be humble in your successes,
and to share in the praises and joy
  of others.
But most of all,
I wish for you to be happy.
For when you are happy,
  you have the key that will open all
    of the world's doors to you.

Whatever you decide,
  whoever you become,
my love for you is unconditional;
my arms and heart are always open to you.
My wishes for you are that you will someday
  know the joys that only a daughter
    can bring
and that all your wishes come true.
I love you, my daughter.

– Jackie Olson

# Daughter, You Are Special

Within you is an ideal,
a voice of youth,
and a promise of achievement
still to come.
Within your hands
    are special gifts and talents.
Within your mind is the
    source of your dreams.
Within you is the strength
to carry your dreams to completion.
Within your heart is the desire
to meet the world on your own terms.
You are strong; you are wise;
you have a dream.
You have a spirit and confidence;
you have faith.
You are your own person,
and you always will be.
Within you is something
so precious and rare.
Within you is the promise
of the future.

— Jean Lamey

"Special" is a word
that is used to describe
something one-of-a-kind
like a hug
or a sunset
or a person who spreads love
with a smile or kind gesture.
"Special" describes people
who act from the heart
and keep in mind the hearts
   of others.
"Special" applies to something
that is admired and precious
and which can never be replaced.
"Special" is the word that best
   describes you.

— Teri Fernandez

# Daughter...

*If ever you need to talk,*
*to share a laugh,*
*a dream, a smile;*
*to be comforted*
*or reassured,*
*to be understood...*

*Remember,*
*my shoulder is there*
*for your head,*
*your secrets are safe*
*and my door*
*is always open.*

*– Ronda Scott*

*I am always here*
*to understand you*
*I am always here*
*to laugh with you*
*I am always here*
*to cry with you*
*I am always here*
*to talk to you*
*I am always here*
*to think with you*
*I am always here*
*to plan with you*
*Even though we*
*might not always*
*be together*
*please know that*
*I am always*
*here to*
*love*
*you*

— Susan Polis Schutz

# Remember This, My Daughter...

*There is no difficulty that enough love will not conquer; No disease that enough love will not heal; No door that enough love will not open; No gulf that enough love will not bridge; No wall that enough love will not throw down; No sin that enough love will not redeem...*

*It makes no difference how deeply seated may be the trouble; How hopeless the outlook; How muddled the tangle; How great the mistake. A sufficient realization of love will dissolve it all... If only you could love enough you would be the happiest and most powerful being in the world.*

*— Emmet Fox*

*Your* success and happiness lie
in you. External conditions are
the accidents of life, its outer
trappings. The great, enduring
realities are love of service. Joy
is the holy fire that keeps
our purpose warm and our
intelligence aglow. Resolve to
keep happy, and your joy and
you shall form an invincible
host against difficulty.

*– Helen Keller*

# For My Beautiful Daughter

*I looked at you today*
*and saw the same beautiful eyes*
*that looked at me with love*
*when you were a baby*
*I looked at you today*
*and saw the same*
*beautiful mouth*
*that made me cry*
*when you first smiled at me*
*when you were a baby*
*It was not long ago*
*that I held you in my arms*
*long after you fell asleep*
*and I just kept rocking you*
*all night long*

I looked at you today
and saw my beautiful daughter
no longer a baby
but a beautiful person
with a full range of emotions
   and feelings
and ideas and goals
Every day is exciting
as I continue to watch you grow
And I want you to always know that
in good and in bad times
I will love you
and that no matter what you do
or how you think
or what you say
you can depend on
my support, guidance
friendship and love
every minute of every day
I love being your mother

– Susan Polis Schutz

# Some Special Wishes
# Just for You

Wishing you a message
  of how special you are.
Today. Tomorrow. And forever.
Wishing you days of celebration.
And favorite people gathered together.

Wishing you wonderful thoughts.
And the best memories anybody ever had.
Wishing you new paths and promises ahead.
And a million reasons to be glad.

Wishing you the warmth of friends and family.
And loved ones always close by.
Wishing you the gifts happiness brings.
And the treasures money can't buy.

Wishing you success and serenity.
And wishes come true.
Wishing you a reminder of how much nicer
  this world is... because of you.

— Casey Whilson

# Daughter, You Are the Most Beautiful Flower in the Garden of My Life

*Like a flower whose petals*
*unfold before my eyes,*
*I watch as you reach out*
*to grab hold of*
*the new opportunities*
*that are coming your way.*
*My little flower...*
*I hope you have been listening*
*to all the things*
*I have tried so hard*
*to impress upon you.*
*Changes and challenges*
*have presented themselves...*
*and you stand ready for anything.*

*Pride is what I feel*
*for this precious flower,*
*as I watch you blossom*
*into a beautiful young woman.*
*You have learned to dream,*
*but more importantly,*
*you have learned to strive*
*toward your goals.*
*You are strong and independent*
*and more beautiful*
*than any flower I have ever seen.*

*– Karen G. Osman*

# A Daughter Is a
# Wonderful Blessing

*A* daughter is one of the greatest
    blessings one could ever have
She begins her life loving and
    trusting you automatically

And for many years, you are
    the center of her life
Together you experience the
    delights of the new things
    she learns and does

You enter into a daughter's play and are once
    again young
And even though it's harder to enter into her
    world as she becomes a teen

You are there, understanding her dilemmas and
    her fears
And wishing with all your heart that she didn't
    have to go through them

A daughter's smile is a precious sight that
    you treasure each time you see it
And the sound of her laughter always brings
    joy to your heart

Her successes mean more to you than your own
And her happiness is your happiness

Her heartaches and disappointments
    become yours, too
Because when she isn't okay, you can't
    be okay either

Daughters aren't perfect, but you come
    close to it
You have given me more happiness
    than you know

I am thankful for your kindness and
    thoughtfulness
And I am proud of who you are
    and how you live your life

Words can't express how much you mean
    to me or how much I love you
The love goes too deep, and the gratitude
    and pride I feel are boundless

Thank you, Daughter, for blessing
    my life in so many ways

                                    – Barbara Cage

*I* want you to know how amazing you are.
*I want you to know how much you're*
*treasured and celebrated and quietly thanked.*

*I want you to feel really good… about who you are.*
*About all the great things you do!*
*I want you to appreciate your uniqueness.*
*Acknowledge your talents and abilities.*
*Realize what a beautiful soul you have.*
*Understand the wonder within.*

*You make so much sun shine through, and you*
*inspire so much joy in the lives of everyone who is*
*lucky enough to know you.*

*You are a very special person, giving so many*
*people a reason to smile. You deserve to receive the*
*best in return, and one of my heart's favorite*
*hopes is that the happiness you give away will*
*come back to warm you*
       *each and every day of your life.*

                 – *Sydney Nealson*

# Always Believe
## in Yourself, Daughter

### ...and Know That You Are Loved

Know yourself –
what you can do
and want to do in life
Set goals
and work hard to achieve them
Have fun every day in every way
Be creative –
it is an expression of your feelings
Be sensitive in viewing the world
Believe in the family
as a stable and rewarding way
of life
Believe in love
as the most complete
and important emotion possible
Believe that you are
an important part of
everyone's life that you touch
Believe in yourself
and know that you are loved

— Susan Polis Schutz

# Fathers and Daughters...

*When a father looks upon a daughter
he bears the love that he bore her mother
echoed down through the years.*

*– Thomas Moore*

*Certain it is that there is no kind
of affection so purely angelic as that
of a father to a daughter. He beholds
her both with and without regard to
her sex. In love to our wives there is
desire; to our sons there is ambition;
but in that to our daughters there is
something which there are no words
to express.*

*– Joseph Addison*

*The lucky man has a daughter as his first child.*

*– Spanish Proverb*

# Mothers and Daughters...

*Mothers of daughters
are daughters of mothers
and have remained so, in
circles joined to circles,
since time began. They
are bound together by
a shared destiny.*

> – Signe Hammer

*Thou art thy mother's glass, and she in thee
Calls back the lovely April of her prime.*

> – William Shakespeare

*Like one, like the other
Like daughter, like mother.*

> – Anonymous

# A Family's Love Can Rise Above Anything That Comes Along

*My dear and wonderful daughter,*
*we all have times*
*when it seems like*
*the sun forgot to shine in our lives*
*and the dreams we were counting*
*so heavily on... forgot how much*
*we wanted them to come true.*

*When you need a place of comfort,*
*a hand to hold, and a heart that cares*
*about your happiness more than words*
*can ever say... remember that you can*
*turn to me... and I'll do whatever*
*I can to help you*
*chase those clouds away.*

*– Ann Turrel*

# *I Am Always Here for You, Daughter...*

When you need someone
to talk to
I hope you will
talk to me
When you need someone
to laugh with
I hope you will
laugh with me
When you need someone
to advise you
I hope you will
turn to me
When you need someone
to help you
I hope you will
let me help you
I cherish and love
everything about you –
my beautiful daughter
And I will always support you
as a mother, as a person
and as a friend

— Susan Polis Schutz

# My Advice
## to You, Daughter...

*Enjoy your life!*
*Laugh a lot. Love a lot.*
*Listen to your heart,*
*and follow where it leads you.*
*Do what you love.*
*Love yourself,*
*and share that love with others.*
*This is the way that we truly*
*make a difference,*
*add our beauty to the world,*
*and give something precious*
*to ourselves and others.*
*You have already*
*made an impression on the world.*
*You have touched my heart*
*and my life*
*in a way that has*
*forever changed me.*
*Thank you for coming into my life,*
*for forgiving any errors I made*
*in raising you,*
*and for allowing me the chance*
*to learn and grow with you.*
*I love you.*

— Donna Newman

*Do* all the good you can,
By all the means you can,
In all the ways you can,
In all the places you can,
At all the times you can,
To all the people you can,
As long as ever you can.

– John Wesley

*Finish* every day and be done with it. For manners and for wise living it is a vice to remember. You have done what you could; some blunders and absurdities no doubt crept in; forget them as soon as you can. To-morrow is a new day; you shall begin it well and serenely, and with too high a spirit to be cumbered with your old nonsense. This day for all that is good and fair. It is too dear, with its hopes and invitations, to waste a moment on... yesterdays.

– Ralph Waldo Emerson
(From a letter to his daughter)

*Always* remember to forget
the things that made you sad,
but never forget to remember
the things that made you glad.

– Elbert Hubbard

# Daughter, You Are
# the Greatest Gift
# I've Ever Received

Memories come
flooding back to me
   as I look back
      over the years.
I want to hold on to you
and at the same time
watch you fly high and free.

You have such spirit
   and a character all your own.
You are a doer and an achiever
   of what you believe in.
I'm so proud of your dreams
   and the conviction you have
to make those dreams come true.
Your world is bright, new,
   and bursting with possibilities.

*It's so easy to remember*
*your very first steps*
*and how I held out my hand*
*for you to hold.*

*As each year passes,*
*you take more steps,*
*and some of these will eventually*
*lead you away from me –*
*but always remember that*
*my hand and my heart*
*are forever here for you.*
*You will always be my daughter,*
*but I have also discovered in you*
*a rare and precious friend.*
*You have been life's greatest gift*
*to me,*
*and I love you so much.*

*– Vickie M. Worsham*

*You have powers you never dreamed of.
You can do things you never thought you
could do. There are no limitations in what
you can do except the limitations in your
own mind as to what you cannot do.
Don't think you cannot.
Think you can.*

— *Darwin P. Kingsley*

*I will support you
in all that you
do
I will help you
in all that you
need
I will share with you
in all that you
experience
I will encourage you
in all that you
try
I will understand you
in all that is in your
heart
I will love you
in all that you
are*

*– Susan Polis Schutz*

# Gentle Words
# of Encouragement

*Spend every day preparing for the next.*

*As you reach forward with one hand, accept the advice of those who have gone before you, and in the same manner reach back with the other hand to those who follow you; for life is a fragile chain of experiences held together by love. Take pride in being a strong link in that chain. Discipline yourself, but do not be harsh. The pleasures of life are yours to be taken. Share them with others, but always remember that you, too, have earned the right to partake.*

*Know those who love you; love is the finest of all gifts and is received only to be given. Embrace those who truly love you; for they are few in a lifetime. Then return that love tenfold, radiating it from your heart to fill their lives as sunlight warms the darkest corners of the earth. Love is a journey, not a destination; travel its path daily. Do this and your troubles will be as fleeting as footprints in the sand. When loneliness is your companion and all about you seem to be gone, pause and listen, for the sound of loneliness is silence, and in silence we hear best. Listen well, and your moments of silence will always be broken by the gentle words of encouragement spoken by those of us who love you.*

*– Tim Murtaugh*

# My Family

There is an
irreplaceable feeling
that I wouldn't give up for the world –
a sense of belonging,
of being able to turn
to the outstretched hands
    of those I love... at any time;
to know they'll understand me,
    and comfort me
    when things go wrong,
or laugh with me
    when things make me happy.
Caring and sharing
    life's ups and downs,
and mostly,
    loving...
as I so dearly love them.

– Debbie Avery Pirus


The family is one of
    nature's masterpieces.

– George Santayana

*You are my daughter, and the meaning of
    that bond between us is boundless.
It means placing your comfort before my own.
It means trying my best every moment of
    every day to shelter you from harm.
It means worrying endlessly, and sometimes
    needlessly, about you and everything that
    enters your life.
It means wanting only the best for you, and
    aching inside at those times when things
    go wrong.
It means giving you all that I have to give
    and feeling your special love fill my
    heart more deeply than I ever imagined.
It means loving you without reserve, and
    with all that I am, for the rest of my life.*

*– Linda Sackett - Morrison*

# Dear Daughter,

*I worry sometimes that I pushed*
  *too hard*
*when you were growing up –*
*wanting so much for you*
*and trying to make sure you had*
*all those things that I didn't*
  *when I was a child.*
*But I hope that I never made you*
*feel that I expected too much…*
*for no matter what you become*
  *or what you achieve,*
*what matters most to me is that*
  *you're happy*
*and that I'm never without your*
  *love.*

*I'll always be here for you…*
  *no matter what you do.*

*– Anna Marie Edwards*

*It is so important
to choose your own
lifestyle
and not let others
choose it for you*

– Susan Polis Schutz

*Do not follow where
the path may lead.
Go, instead, where
there is no path
and leave a trail.*

– Anonymous

# Hold Fast Your Dreams

Hold fast your dreams!
Within your heart
Keep one still, secret spot
Where dreams may go,
And, sheltered so,
May thrive and grow
Where doubt and fear are not.
O keep a place apart,
Within your heart,
For little dreams to go!

Think still of lovely things that are not true.
Let wish and magic work at will in you.
Be sometimes blind to sorrow. Make believe!
Forget the calm that lies
In disillusioned eyes.
Though we all know that we must die,
Yet you and I
May walk like gods and be
Even now at home in immortality.

*We see so many ugly things –*
*Deceits and wrongs and quarrelings;*
*We know, alas! we know*
*How quickly fade*
*The color in the west,*
*The bloom upon the flower,*
*The bloom upon the breast*
*And youth's blind hour.*
*Yet keep within your heart*
*A place apart*
*Where little dreams may go,*
*May thrive and grow.*
*Hold fast – hold fast your dreams!*

*– Louise Driscoll*

*When the world closes in*
*and lies so heavily upon you...*
*remember that I care.*
*When the ones with whom you*
*share your life seem like strangers...*
*remember that I care.*
*When love seems to only bring*
*you pain...*
*remember that I care.*
*What cannot be, cannot be.*
*But always remember, I care.*
*Never be afraid to come to me,*
*if you have need of the*
*    simplest thing.*
*No matter what it is...*
*                    I care.*

*– Kathy Boss*

*i* wish for you warmth
when it is cold outside

i wish for you a star
when the night is dark

i wish for you courage
when the world is afraid

i think of you, i wish for you
and i hope you know –
that here, there is a heart
and a home;
and here, there is someone
who loves you
more than any wish could
      ever give.

– laura west rosenthal

# Child of Mine

*It's been so gratifying*
*for me to see you*
*go through such positive changes*
*and inner growth.*
*Your happiness is contagious,*
*and I'm so happy for you...*
*to see you becoming*
*a strong individual*
*and doing all the right things*
*to make your days ahead*
*shine even brighter.*

*It's been great for me*
*to watch you grow*
*and to become*
*even more of that special someone*
*you are... inside.*

*Through your growing and changing,*
*I want to ask that you*
  *take me along with you.*
*I don't mean that I want you*
*to tell me every thought*
  *you have along the way,*
*but to remember that I am here...*
  *wherever and whenever you need me.*
*And I hope that you'll remember*
  *that I'm on your side.*
*And even if I can't always help you win,*
*there will never be a day*
  *when I won't be*
      *cheering you on.*

*– Laine Parsons*

*My darling daughter*
*I am so glad that*
*you were born today*
*when women are so*
*aware of what is going on*
*and don't always have*
*to fight so hard to be heard*
*The world is wide open*
*for you to be whatever you want*
*It will be hard*
*but at least you*
*will find other women*
*striving for the same things*
*and you won't be called "crazy"*
*for wanting to achieve them*
*Though full equality*
*is a long way off*
*there certainly have been changes*
*which would make your life as a woman*
*not so stereotyped and confined*
*My darling daughter*
*you are living in an age*
*where womanhood is finally growing*
*to be everything*
*that it can be*

*— Susan Polis Schutz*

# Believe in Yourself, and Live Your Life with Thankfulness for All the Gifts You've Been Given

*You* have the ability to become
all you are capable
of becoming.
Forget problems
that don't matter anymore
and worries that will wash away
on the shore of tomorrow.
Determine your own worth
by yourself,
and do not be dependent
on another's judgment of you.
Dare to dream,
and live those dreams,
for it is then
that you can begin to realize
your true destiny.
Live life fully
with thankfulness and joy
for all the gifts
you've been given.

— Debbi Oehman

# More Than You Know...
## Daughter

*I'd like to tell you*
*how much I love you,*
*and I hope you know that I do...*
*I wish that the words I speak*
*    so gently to you could be*
*heard by your heart*
*    with the same meanings*
*and the same soft feelings of love*
*that they carry from deep within me.*

*For more than you know...*
*    I love so many things about you.*
*    I enjoy sharing life with you.*
*I enjoy the way we balance each other out,*
*how we share the good times*
*    and support each other through the tears...*

I enjoy the knowledge that we'll make it
   through whatever life brings
with courage and with love
through the years.

More than you know...
   and more than I can ever say,
I feel a wonderful thankfulness
   in my heart... just for you.
And I want you to remember, though
   my thoughts don't always convey
   and my feelings don't always show,
I love you, and I always will...
   more than you know.

— Andrew Tawney

# I'm Fortunate to Have a Daughter
# Who Is Also My Friend

You must know that I love you
and that I am proud you are my daughter,
but I may have failed to let you know
how I feel about you as a person.
When you were young, it seemed as if
I was constantly busy taking care of you
and trying to keep up with
the demands of raising a child.
Yet you were always my greatest joy.
In time, it seemed as if our roles somehow became reversed,
and you returned my devotion
by letting me lean on you.
There were times when you seemed
so wise for your years
that I caught a glimpse of the woman
you would someday become.
Now you are that woman,
and I'm proud that you are my daughter.
But you are also a very special person
who has filled my life with a precious, ever-growing friendship.
You are my dearest friend –
one who is loving, kind, and compassionate.
You support me at all times by giving your time and love;
I know I can count on you to always be there.
You listen to my problems
with quiet understanding, and through you
I am often able to find solutions.
You are my biggest fan
when I have achieved a personal goal,
sharing my triumphs with pride and affection.
I love you because you are my daughter,
but I also love you for the very special person you are.

— Lori Pike

# I Think of You
# Every Day

*You probably don't realize how important you are to me. There are times when the one thing that helps me get through the day... is thinking of you.*

*You bring happiness to me when the world seems to be wearing a frown. When things don't quite go as planned and my world seems upside down, my thoughts of you help to set things right again.*

*You are so important to me.*
*You make me think, you make me laugh, you make me feel alive. You put things in perspective for me. You provide support and encouragement, you lessen my worries, and you increase my joys. If my life were a puzzle, you would be the one piece that was a perfect fit.*

*Every day... I think of you.*
*And I've got a million smiles to prove it.*

*— Marin McKay*

# Daughter, You Are So Precious to Me

*When you came into this world and into my life, so many beautiful things happened. Although I was the one holding you, you were the one enfolding so many of my hopes and dreams. Although I was the one who was supposed to teach you all the things to do as you grew up, you were the one who taught me — constantly — of my capacity to love, to experience life in its most meaningful way, and to open my heart wide enough to let all those joyful feelings inside.*

*If ever you wonder if anyone cares, know that the love I have for you transcends time and bridges any distance imaginable. Remember: If you ever need me, I will <u>always</u> be there... Nothing will ever be as strong as my love and my thankfulness... for you.*

*— Laurel Atherton*

*Even
if a day
should go by
when I don't say
"I love you..."*

*May never a
moment go by
without you
knowing I do*

*– Daniel Haughian*

# A Wish for You,
# My Daughter

*If there could be only one thing
in life for me to teach you,
I would teach you to love...*

*To respect others so that you may
find respect in yourself
To learn the value of giving,
so that if ever there comes a time
in your life when someone is really in
need, you will give
To act in a manner that you would
wish to be treated; to be proud
of yourself
To laugh and smile as much as you
can, in order to help bring joy
back into this world
To have faith in others;
to be understanding
To stand tall in this world and
to learn to depend on yourself*

*To only take from this earth*
  *those things which you really*
  *need, so there will be enough*
  *for others*
*To not depend on money or*
  *material things for your*
  *happiness, but*
*To learn to appreciate the people*
  *who love you, the simple beauty*
  *that God gave you and to find*
  *peace and security within*
  *yourself*

*To you, my child, I hope I have*
  *taught all of these things,*
  *for they are love.*

*— Donna Dargis*

# To My Daughter

Since you were born
you have been
such a beautiful
addition to our family
Now that you are growing up
I can see that
you are a beautiful
addition to the world
and I am so
proud of you

*As we watch you*
*doing things on your own*
*we know you will find*
*happiness and success*
*because we are confident in*
*your ability*
*your self-knowledge*
*your values*
*But if you ever need a boost*
*or just someone to talk to*
*about difficulties that might be occurring*
*we are always here*
*to help you*
*to understand you*
*to support you*
*and to love*
*you*

— Susan Polis Schutz

# Daughter

Goals are dreams and wishes
that are not easily reached.
You have to work hard to
    obtain them,
never knowing when
    or where
you will reach your goal.

But keep trying!
Do not give up hope.
And most of all...
never stop
    believing in yourself.

For within you
there is someone
    special...

someone wonderful
    and successful.
No matter what you achieve,
as long as you want it
    and it makes you
        happy,

    you are a success.

— Rosemary DePaolis

# My Darling Daughter

*You are a shining
example of what a
daughter can be –
love and laughter
beautiful and good
honest and principled
determined and independent
sensitive and intelligent
You are a shining
example of what every
mother wishes her
daughter were
and I
am so very
proud of
you*

*— Susan Polis Schutz*

# Daughter,
# You Have Given Me
# Happiness and Smiles

You are a blessing
that I'm forever thankful for.
I love being with you,
and every time we're apart
there's a little part of me
that stays with you.

Your sense of humor delights me.
Your laughter is one of
    my favorite sounds,
and your smiles light up my heart.

I'm so proud of you
and the kind of person you are.
People know they can count on you.
You go out of your way for others
and make a difference in the lives
    of those you care about.
You're helpful to others,
and you are independent, as well.
I'm very pleased with all
you've accomplished on your own.

I love you,
and I want you to know
that being your parent
has been one of my greatest joys.

— Barbara Cage

# Carry This Thought in Your Heart Forever...

*If I could stand beside you always,*
*I would.*
*If I could carry you over all the obstacles,*
*I would.*
*If I could turn all your tears to laughter,*
*I would.*
*If I could tell you*
*all that will happen to you,*
*I would.*
*But I can only tell you*
*one thing with certainty:*
*I love you.*
*And I hope my love will*
*shine on all your tomorrows*
*and brighten every step*
*you take in the future.*

*– Dorothy Hewitt*